Introducing
Singing

Pieces, exercises and tips for the beginner singer

by Ben Vonberg-Clark

Published by
Trinity College London Press Ltd
trinitycollege.com
Registered in England
Company no. 09726123
Copyright © 2023 Trinity College London Press Ltd
First impression, March 2023

Printed in England by Halstan & Co Ltd, Amersham, Bucks

Contents

For information on accessing the audio and animations see inside back cover.

Introduction

To Charlotte, Oskar and Egon – the home team

Welcome to this book and to your singing journey. I hope that you will use it to start to discover the true potential of your voice and the huge range of expression that it can achieve. If you are a teacher, I hope that this will be a helpful resource and that the exercises and songs will prove a useful addition to your beginners' repertoire. If you are looking through this on your own, work through it slowly and in order. Try not to rush and don't force your voice to do things that don't come naturally. The audio material and animations should help you along your way. Enjoy!

Handy tips

- Like training any muscle in the gym, your voice and support muscles will take time to build in strength. Be patient and it will come.

- Don't try to sound like someone else – your voice is *your* voice and you should be proud of it.

- I don't believe that people are 'tone deaf' – it's more likely that your muscles are unfamiliar with the singing sensation. You can do this!

3

Stage 1 – The Basics

This first stage covers the basics of music notation. It is not necessary to read music to use this book, as many of the concepts are to do with how you make the sound and what your body is doing, and when you do come across notation, there will often be an audio track for you to listen to.

It may seem daunting if you are new to notation, but take each section slowly and gradually the ideas should become clearer. You could think of this section as more of a reference section as you progress through this book. For those that perhaps already play another instrument, much of this section should be familiar to you, and so serves as a reminder.

The Stave

Music is usually written on a set of five lines called a **stave**.

The **note-heads** (the oval-shaped dots shown below) can be put either on the lines, like this:

Or in the spaces between the lines, like this:

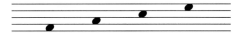

To show exactly which high or low sound to play, each sound has a name.
The letters used to name notes are **A B C D E F G.** They repeat themselves over and over again – higher and higher.
A **treble clef** (or G clef) is used for high notes. The little curved line in the middle of the clef curls around the second line where the note **G** sits:

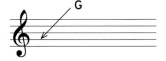

High notes are written near the top of the stave and **low notes** near the bottom.
The lines coming from the note-heads are called **stems**.
As a general rule, if the notes are high the stems go down and if the notes are low the stems go up. The middle line is usually the only line where a stem can go up or down. This makes the music easy to read.

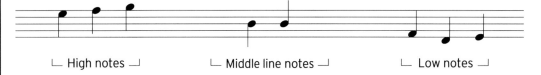

Here are the most common treble clef notes you may come across:

Lines and Spaces

Treble clef lines:

Treble clef spaces:

You may like to think of words to help you remember these (for example, **E**very **G**reen **B**us **D**rives **F**ast).

Note and Rest values

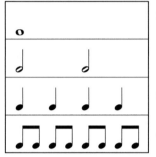

Semibreve This note lasts for four crotchet beats

Minims These notes last for two crotchet beats each

Crotchets These notes last for one crotchet beat each

Quavers These notes last for half a crotchet beat each.

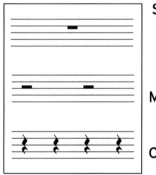

Semibreve rest This rest lasts for four crotchet beats
or
a whole bar of silence in any time signature

Minim rests These rests last for two crotchet beats each

Crotchet rests These rests last for one crotchet beat each

Bars and Barlines

Beats are organised into **bars**, with a **barline** at the end of each one. The first beat of the bar is usually a little stronger than the others and this adds a particular character to the music:

2-crotchet bars

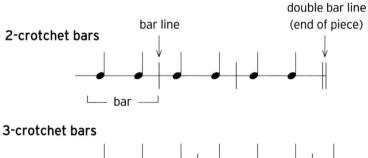

3-crotchet bars

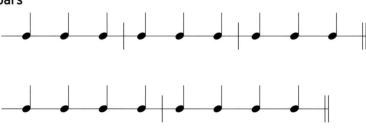

Time Signatures

There is a **time signature** at the beginning of the music.

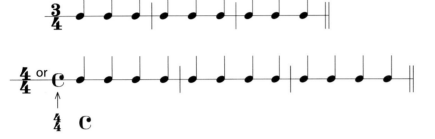

The top number of a time signature shows the number of beats in a bar

The bottom number shows the type of beat in a bar (4 means crotchet)

Slurs

When we sing, sometimes each syllable has only one note attached to it. The song 'Happy Birthday' is a good example of that. Have a little sing of it and you'll see what I mean.

Other songs **spread the syllables out a bit** – sometimes a syllable has two notes, sometimes three or, in some operas, more like 53. **Slurs** are what join these notes together:

If you think of the national anthem, it's mainly **syllabic** – one note per syllable. When you get right to the end, however, the last 'God' has **two** notes – and these are joined by a slur. Remember this, it will be very useful when you are singing music from the page.

This song is based on the Christmas carol 'O little Town of Bethlehem'. The melody repeats itself twice. Listen to the audio and spot the slurs.

Track 1

Sing Each Morning

Sing each mor‑ning, sing_ all_ night and_ that will_ do you good!

If you want to sing_ all_ day, then_ we'll re‑ply: you should!

Stage 2 – Start To Vocalise!

We all know people who say that they cannot sing, yet these same people use their voices to lead, encourage, calm and excite others every day. Moving your voice from speaking to singing is not such a big gear change. Don't think too much and follow the exercises below:

 ## Speaking into singing

The main difference between speaking and singing is the length of the **vowels** and the **consonants**. Let's take a simple word: food. Say the word '**food**' a few times, nice and slowly. Now isolate each component:

FFFFF-OOOOOOOOO-D

> 'F' is created by your **upper teeth on your bottom lip**. Let some air through. Do this a few times.

> 'OO' comes by pushing your lips forward into a **circle like a fish** and allowing air through.

> 'D' comes by popping the tip of your tongue to the roof of your mouth at the same time as a puff of air.

> Go through all three steps in a row, exaggerating each one. Really enjoy the long 'ooo' vowel. Now you're singing!

 ## Coughing and laughing

Go ahead and have a cough whilst putting your hands around your belly button – try not to aim at someone...! What happens? Does your belly go in and out? Now have a laugh. Think of something really funny – a cat riding a skateboard – anything – and see what those muscles do. They'll be naturally responding, supporting your laughter. **Remember that feeling – these are your singing muscles.**

 ## Sobbing and crying

Have you ever seen a dog waiting longer than expected for food? What sound do they make? Keeping your lips together, try to **imitate the sob of a dog**. What happens in your body? Can you feel the sound coming from the centre of your rib cage as it expands and contracts? Can you now expand this into a good old cry? Have a good sob about something. **You should feel your belly and rib cage expanding and contracting.** This is good: you are well on the way to healthy singing.

Warming Up

Like any physical activity, it's important to warm up before you start. Your vocal cords are only about 4mm thick, so you need to be gentle with them as you get going. The exercises below, especially humming, are very effective at getting your voice into gear in a gentle way. For extending your warm up, you can use the interval exercises on pages 18-20.

 ## Humming

Imagine you have just **put a strawberry into your mouth** and you don't want anyone to see: your teeth stay apart, but you close your lips. Feel the **space in your mouth** where the imaginary strawberry sits, breathe in through your nose and start to hum. Sing whatever note comes out naturally. Once you run out of breath, breathe in through your nose and hum again.

After you have done this three times, start to play around with the hum – can you go lower? Can you go up and down, whilst keeping your head still? Play around with this and enjoy the vibrations of your voice through your body.

 ## nnnnggggg

Now gently part your lips and encourage the back of your tongue up to the roof of your mouth. This will create an 'ng' sound, and the air will come out of your nose. Breathe in, make a sound. Repeat and play with these new sensations.

Stage 3 – Awareness Of Your Body

Where do you sing from? From your neck? Make a noise with your fingers pressed on the front of your neck. You might have heard this called the 'Adam's Apple' – that is where our sound is made – our **vocal folds**. These folds are so small, we need to use the **whole of our body** to help support them to make sound. We use our **bellies**, **ribs**, **knees**, **shoulders**, **ankles**, **feet** and everything in between.

Many singers, therefore, do some **simple stretches** before they start singing to make sure their bodies are relaxed and able to support their singing.

> **Safety warning!**
> Make sure you have a teacher or parent observe you when you do these stretches for the first time — you need to look after your body!

 **Loosening up**

◗ Scrunch up your toes and release them.

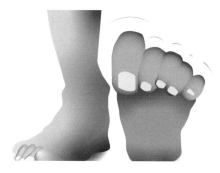

◗ Rock backwards and forwards from your heels to the balls of your feet. Find your centre of balance.

◗ Rotate your waste round in circles slowly, first anti-clockwise and then clockwise. Note where the centre point is.

◗ Hug yourself tightly, feeling the stretch in your ribs behind you.

9

Reach up to the ceiling and give your fingers a wiggle.

Squeeze your shoulders up and hold them there for **5 seconds**. When you release them you will **feel amazing**.

Roll your tongue around in a circle inside your mouth, like you are **clearing out your dinner from your teeth**. Then go the other way.

Make your face as big as possible, and then as small as possible, scrunching it right up.

Posture – animation

Here is a **five-step process** to help set up and maintain a healthy posture. Watch the video to check that you are doing it correctly.

Start with your feet together, shoulders forward and head bowed facing the ground.

▶ Move **one foot away from the other one**, just wider than hip-distance apart

▶ Tuck your **pelvis forwards** so that it is lined up underneath your rib-cage

▶ **Squeeze your shoulders up** to your ears and hold them there

▶ **Release your shoulders** and let your breath out

▶ Allow your **head to float upwards** and relax your chin

In the following song, you will see a few markings you may not have seen before. Sometimes a composer needs to tell the performer how loudly or softly to sing. This is done by adding dynamics above the stave. Here are a list of the most common dynamics you may come across:

Dynamics

pp (*pianissimo*) means sing very softly
p (*piano*) means sing softly
mp (*mezzo piano*) means sing moderately softly
mf (*mezzo forte*) means sing moderately loudly
f (*forte*) means sing loudly
ff (*fortissimo*) means sing very loudly

Crescendo means getting gradually louder
You may also see the word *cresc.* or the symbol: ————

Diminuendo means getting gradually softer.
You may also see the words *dim.* or *decresc.*, or the symbol: ————

You will also see phrase marks and breath marks in the next song.

A **phrase mark** is a curved line written over the notes and is there to encourage smooth singing without breathing between the notes.

The **breath mark** is often written as a 'tick' and shows you when to breathe. if there are no rests between phrases, you can slightly shorten the note before the breath mark, to make sure you have time for a healthy breath.

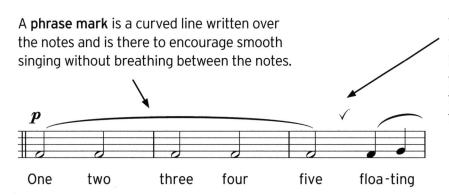

One   two   three   four   five   floa-ting

When you sing each number, use the actions of the **five-step posture exercise** shown previously. Allow each movement to roll into the next one.

Tracks 2&3

The Posture Song

Ben Vonberg-Clark

Stay right there, and feel li - ghter than air.

Sing-ing is ea-sy, you feel bright and bree-zy, when you feel you're floa-ting

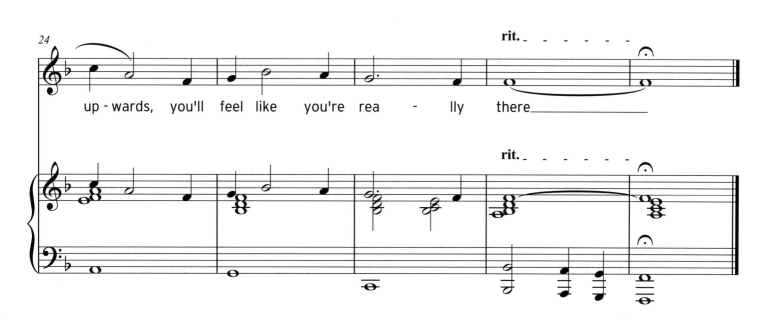

up - wards, you'll feel like you're rea - lly there

Here are some extended posture exercises and thoughts that build on the previous simpler exercises:

Rib Cage

Our rib cage expands naturally when we breathe in. Here are two classic stretches to develop this:

- Hold your elbows with the opposite hand (like you are hugging an imaginary someone) and bring your arms perpendicular to the floor. Keeping your head facing forwards, rotate from the waist to the right and hold, and then to the left.

- Interlock your fingers and push your palms away from you, and then up to the ceiling. Lean over to the right, bending from the waist, and then to the left. When you repeat, you should feel the distance you can lean increase.

Shoulders

Children and adults spend so much time in front of a screen now, so shoulder tension is incredibly common. Use these stretches as much as possible:

- Hug yourself, tightly clasping your arms across your body. This should allow your shoulder blades to drift apart. Then do the opposite: squeeze your shoulder blades together, like you are trying to squash a banana between them. Repeat and increase the range of motion the second time.

- Rotate your shoulders backwards and forwards. Press your shoulders backwards and imagine you are holding a plum between your shoulder blades. Release and repeat.

- Stand side-on to a wall and place your hand on it with your fingers facing backwards. Gently rotate your body until you feel a stretch at the front of your shoulder.

Neck

- Look over your right shoulder, keeping your shoulders facing forwards.

- Same on the left side, and repeat.

- Rotate your head gently round in a clockwise direction, and then anticlockwise.

- Do this slowly and be kind to yourself.

The Jaw

One other thing we need to do is to keep our jaw free and relaxed. Some people open their mouths and hold them there like they are trying to chew a rock or seriously stale baguette. We want to allow our jaw to melt downwards and backwards, as you can see in this animation.

 The Jaw – animation`

Stage 4 – Breathing

We take our first breath as babies. In fact, babies really are rather good at breathing and using their muscles correctly to create some serious volume after they are born. When you hear people talking about breathing in connection with singing, you will often hear them talk about the **diaphragm**. This is the muscle that **draws air into your lungs** when it contracts and **releases the air** when it relaxes. This will continue to operate **without you thinking about it** – what concerns us is using surrounding muscles to help us use our inhaled air efficiently.

There are some noises that we make instinctively that use our **support muscles** in the right way. Have a go at some:

◗ Coughing

◗ Sneezing

◗ Sobbing

◗ Sounds of shock or surprise (Whoa!!)

◗ Sighing

> ### Handy tip
> Try not to cough into your teacher's face as you are doing this!

You should feel the muscles in your tummy contract and move inwards towards your spine when you cough. Sneezing will be the same, but more exaggerated.

Breathing *in* therefore should be the opposite process – we want to feel our belly inflating when we breathe in.

The next time you see a **cat or dog curled up when asleep**, take a look at how it is breathing. You will see its relaxed body expand and the rib cage float outwards when it breathes in, and the whole body deflates when breathing out.

What we need to do is replicate this – so **find somewhere comfortable to lie down on your back** and we can work on our breathing.

  ## Breathing naturally

Put a book under your head and pull your feet towards you, bend your knees and place your feet flat on the floor. Once you are lying safely on your back put your hands on your tummy, just below your bellybutton. Focus on your breathing, **breathing in through your nose and out through your mouth.** When you breathe in, your hands and belly should **rise up towards the ceiling**, and when you breathe out your hands should **move down towards the floor.** Repeat this until it feels like second nature – **up** when you breathe **in, down** when you breathe **out.**
Watch the animation video to check things out.

> ### Did you know?
>
> Breathing IN your belly gets BIGGER
> Breathing OUT your belly gets SMALLER

> ### Safety warning!
> Breathing in this way, until you get used to it, can make you feel light-headed. After a while of practicing breathing in this way it will start to feel normal, but it's a good reason to practice this exercise lying down to begin with.

It's possible to use these exercises as a basis, and vary them with the following combinations:

Breathing Exercises

Breathing in through your mouth, and out:

- To a **hissing** sound (sssssss)

- To a **zzzzzzzz** (adding a note to the sssssss)

- To **shhhhhhhh**

- To a **jjjjjjjj** (adding a note to the shhhhhhhh)

- To a **ffffffff**

- To a **vvvvvvvv** (adding a note to the ffffffff)

These are known as 'unvoiced' and 'voiced' consonants.

You can then change the ratio between inhalation and exhalation:

- Breathe in for 4 beats, and then out for 4 beats

- Breathe in for 2 beats and out for 6

- Breathe in for 1 beat and out for 7

One final idea

Push out all the breath out of your body and hold your breath for 4 seconds. Then release your tummy and the breath should pop into your body. This is a wonderful feeling that is entirely natural and is something we should try to replicate when we sing.

Many singers forget to breathe usefully before, or indeed during a song. This tune has rests deliberately built in – to remind you to breathe! You can sing it a few times, change the tempo around and you can change key, with the help of your teacher.

Tracks 4&5

If You Want to Sing

Ben Vonberg-Clark

Stage 5 – Developing The voice

The Major Scale and Intervals

The major scale is a series of 8 notes that proceed upwards (or downwards) in step. The distance between the bottom note and the top note is called an octave, as they are eight notes apart.

The following exercises help us get familiar with the scale, and we can see how tunes can be made out of it by using smaller parts of the scale (we call these intervals).

Sing the exercises below in the following order:

1. humming
2. to an 'ng'
3. to an 'ah' vowel
4. With some words – I have suggested some options

Handy tip

There are many other sounds available, such as rolling your lips, rolling your 'r's, vvvvv, zzzzz – your teacher may have other favourites they like to use too.

Try not to disconnect your breath through each phrase. It helps if you slightly slide between the notes.
You can sing this in any key but it helps to start lower down in your vocal range.

Track 6   Intervals – 2nds

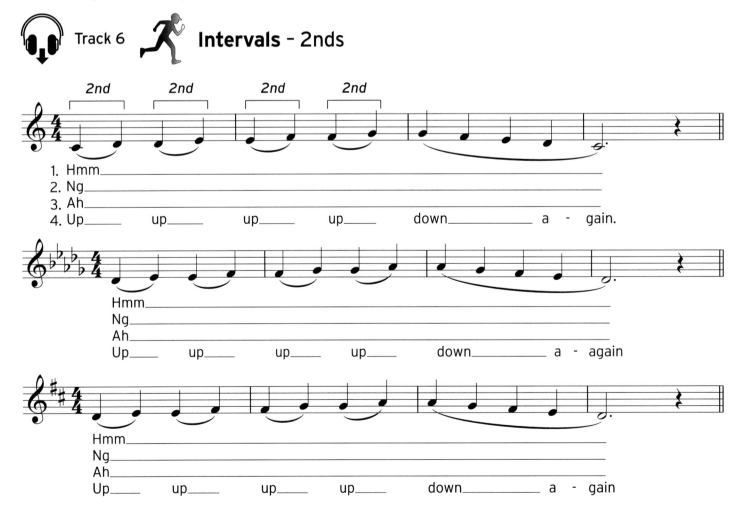

18

Intervals – 3rds

Intervals – 4ths

Intervals - 5ths

Hmm_____
Ng_____
Ah_____
Hmm_____ 5 4 3 2 1

The following tune can help us get familiar with the scale and intervals.

Tracks 10&11

Which Pitch?

Ben Vonberg-Clark

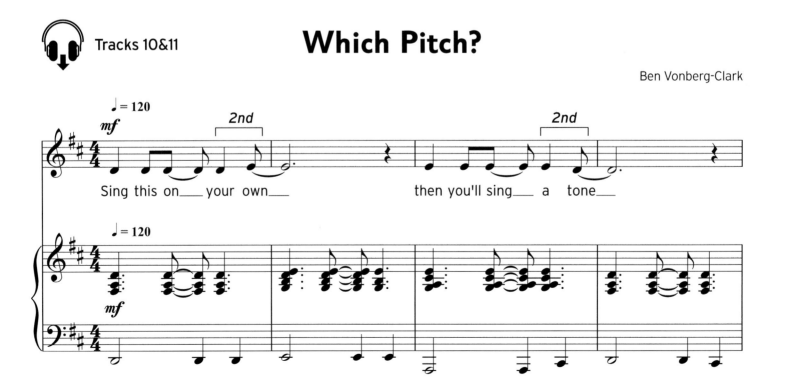

Sing this on___ your own___ then you'll sing___ a tone___

Expanding your range – Arpeggios

The major arpeggio has the same notes as the major scale, but has some left out. When we talk about the 'major triad' this refers to the first three notes of the arpeggio (1, 3 & 5). These notes are used to form a major chord when sounded at the same time.

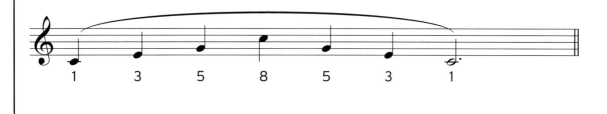

1   3   5   8   5   3   1

When we speak, most of us only use a **tiny little bit** of our voices. This makes sense, as it would be quite unsettling for our friends and family if we constantly bombarded them with **random notes and volumes** (although that's quite fun sometimes!).

However when we sing, our voices can be FREE! Here are a series of exercises that you can sing with your teacher to help get your voice moving and using more of its range. Here are a series of exercises that use the major triad/ arpeggio as its basis, and encourage vocal agility and expansion of the vocal range.

Track 12   Major triad

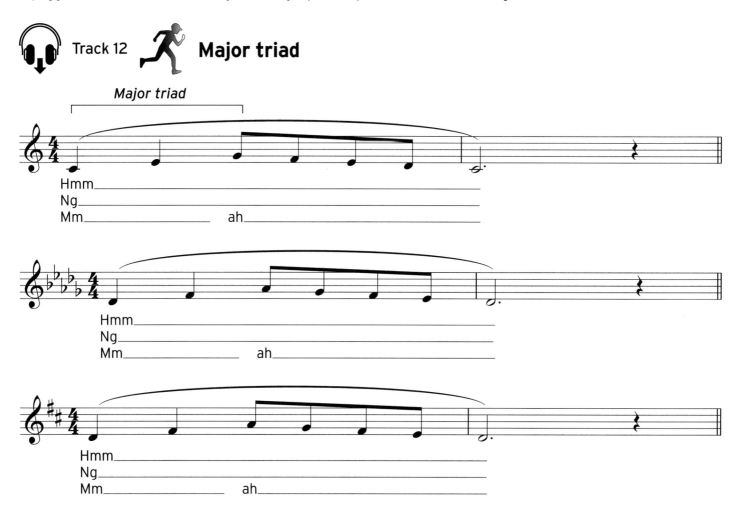

 Track 13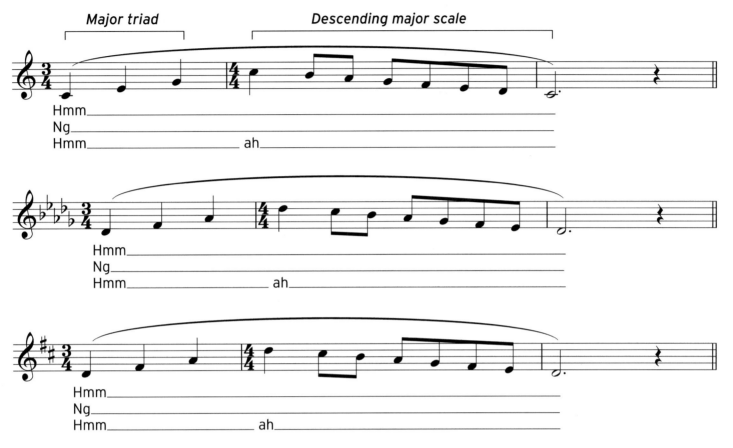

Major arpeggio/descending major scale

You may notice that your voice feels different when singing different pitches. You may feel that your voice 'clicks into different gears' when you are singing a scale or an arpeggio. Do not worry about this, as this is entirely normal.

Most of us speak in the **bottom third of our vocal range**, and our vocal muscles are therefore most used to these pitches and are most comfortable there. When required to sing pitches outside of this range, some people can feel discomfort as they try to force their speaking voice beyond its capability. It's for this reason that many people believe that they 'cannot sing'.

It is like trying to **drive down the motorway at 70 miles per hour in second gear** – you might manage it but your car may explode! One of the most common songs that we all sing reinforces this – 'Happy Birthday'. It starts simply enough, but by the time we get to the third 'happy birthday', we have to leap **eight whole notes**.

One of kindest ways to navigate the octave is to slide between the notes, keeping our shoulders down, head still and our jaws relaxed. You can do this to a hum, an 'ng' sound, or open up to a vowel of your choice. Do this slowly, and get comfortable with it.

Track 14 **Octave leap**

After you are happy with the octave leap, you can then tackle this next exercise:

Track 15   **Octaves/descending major scale**

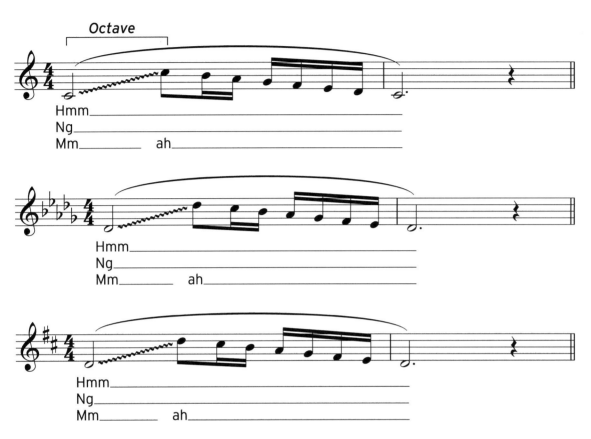

Many popular songs contain the interval of an octave. Aside from 'Happy Birthday, we have 'Somewhere over the Rainbow', 'Singin' in the Rain' and the chorus of 'Let it Snow'. The best way to do this is to use your different vocal 'gears'. Instead of forcing your speaking voice upwards (you may have heard this called the 'chest voice'), you could try employing your second gear. Think of it like a **trampoline** rather than climbing up a ladder: use the lower note to bounce your voice upwards and land on the top note, rather than dragging your voice upwards, which will make it tighter and more tense.

My favourite song to practise this is called 'As the Swan Sings', as the upper note has a gentle 'ooo' vowel which makes a lovely, gentle rounded sound and is especially suitable for singing in your upper register.

Track 16   **As the Swan Sings**

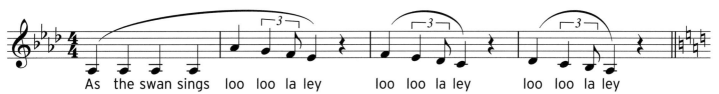

As   the swan sings   loo   loo   la ley   loo   loo   la ley   loo   loo   la ley

If you are happy with this, we can change key and sing the same song in a different part of your vocal register.

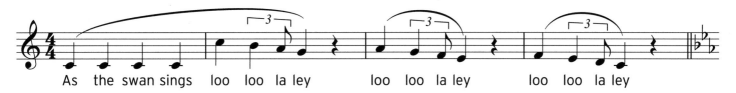

As   the swan sings   loo   loo   la ley   loo   loo   la ley   loo   loo   la ley

It may be that at this point your voice wants to 'change gear'.

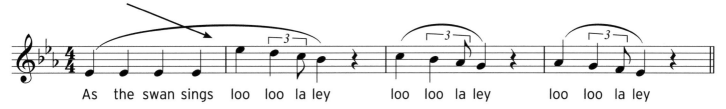

As   the swan sings   loo   loo   la ley   loo   loo   la ley   loo   loo   la ley

Remember

When 'changing gear', allow it to happen, keep your shoulders down and your jaw and neck relaxed. If it's tricky, remember to hum the interval, sliding between the notes. Remember to push your lips forward to the 'ooo' vowel.

Stage 6 – Fun Songs To Work On

Here are some songs for you to have a go at. Some of them are new songs and some traditional folk melodies. Listen to the audio tracks and have a go at learning your favourites. If you feel comfortable, why not have a go at singing them to your friends or family?

In this first song you will see that some notes have been 'tied' together, which in this song makes a really fun rhythm, called syncopation. Listen to the audio to get an idea of how it should go.

Ties

Sometimes composers want musicians to play or sing notes that are not of a standard length. To do this they 'tie' same-pitch notes together to make longer notes.

Here is an **F** that lasts for eight crotchet beats. Notice that the note is tied across the bar line:

4   +   4   =   8 crotchet beats

Tracks 17&18

We're Singing Well

Ben Vonberg-Clark

We're sin-ging well___ we've heard the call,___ we're

free, but most___ of all with shoul-ders back___ and feet a - part___ we're

fee - ling   eight   feet   tall_____ We're

sin - ging   we   are   sin - ging   You   can't

stop   us   if   you   try_____

You don't need many notes to create a song, as demonstrated here. Character and clarity of text is often far more important to create an engaging performance. One way that composers convey character is to use articulations such as accents or tenutos.

An **accent** (>) requires you to sing that note with more force or attack. When singing, this can turn into shouting if you're not careful, so it's best to use the consonant to create the accent – a nice 'w' at the start of bar six, for example.

A straight line above a note is called a **tenuto** (see bar nine). This encourages a singer to 'ooze' as much length out of a note as possible. This creates more emphasis and makes the music more interesting.

Tracks 19&20

The Litter Song

Ben Vonberg-Clark

Crisp pa-ckets, sweet wra-ppers, yes-ter-day's rice! Oo-zing all o-ver the road as

food for the mice! Give me that sack right there and let's get to work!

We are the li-tter pi-ckers and we're not go-nna smirk! Look a-round you

What you go-nna do? Streets free from li-tter look good: You know it's true!

Longing for Peace

Ben Vonberg-Clark

This folk song was collected in c. 1900 near where I come from in Chelmsford, Essex. I remember finding if funny when I was younger. It is also helpful to learn as it really gets us familiar with all the notes of the major scale. Play around with the dynamics on each verse, and enjoy the characters of the queen and the miller.

Tracks 23&24

Good King Arthur

Trad.
arr. Ben Vonberg-Clark

4. The king and queen had scarce sat down, to take their morning meal,
   When at the door a knock, a voice, 'Who stole my morning meal?!'

5. The queen stepped out and on her fork she held a tempting slice,
   'Oh miller dear, do taste of this, you'll find it very nice!'

6. Then every day a bag of meal was sent up to the king,
   The miller too, each morning came, to taste the fried pudding.

Troubleshooting

Voice cracking

You may attempt to sing a note and it may not some out in the way you planned. This is normal and it is nothing to worry about, and can happen often when the voice changes and evolves during adolescence. Remember not to force anything and sing as smoothly as you can.

Lack of power

Like any sport, power and volume come with time and practice. When singing alongside other people it can be very tempting to overdo it, as you cannot really hear yourself properly. In singing, it is sometimes easier to think about how your voice feels to you, rather than how loud it sounds. Be patient.

Voice feels tired

This can happen to all of us. Many people constantly drink water to try to soothe this, or suck huge amounts of sweets and pastels. This tactic will only work well in the short-term. Healthy breathing and neck, tongue and a jaw free of tension is the only way to avoid this. (Staying generally hydrated is, of course, important).
Remember, we use our voices all the time when not singing too – how we speak has a huge impact on the health of our voice. Try to **avoid screaming or shouting**, and try and **support your speaking voice** in much the same way as your singing voice.

I have a cold

Provided a cold has not affected your vocal folds or gone down into your chest, it may be possible to sing with a slight head cold. If your sinuses are blocked you may lose some of your resonance, but it can be done. In a post-covid world, this may, however, be best done at home!

Nerves make it difficult for me to sing

Many of us get nervous when we sing and some nerves can be very helpful, making you alert and giving you the energy required for performance. Too many nerves may make things a little difficult, but there are some ways to lower your heart rate, and they centre on breathing. Breathing **slowly in through your nose, and out through your mouth**. This won't, of course, work for everyone all of the time.

I don't sound like my singing hero/idol

We are all born with our own voice that sounds unique to us. There is, of course, an element of consistency between voices that we do desire – an unforced tone that sounds free and easy – but if you try to sound too much like someone else, performances **can come across as false** and you could harm your voice by trying to make it something that is isn't. **Be proud of your own voice.**

My voice can sound 'breathy'

This is very common and can happen when the vocal chords do not meet fully and air can escape between them. We want to help the chords meet fully. The exercises on pages 18-20 singing to 'ng' are the safest and quickest way to prevent air escaping and to help the chords meet effectively.
During adolescence, the voice changes and evolves along with other changes in your body. This can result in breathiness, particularly in your upper register. This is extremely normal and will settle down as your body matures.

My voice gets tired when I sing softly

It is common in choirs to be asked to sing softly, and we often see *piano* (*p*) in the dynamics in solo songs. The problem is that many of us switch off our support muscles instinctively to sing quietly, like we are trying to keep a secret from someone. This leaves our **tiny vocal folds** with no backup, a lot of breath can escape and we can quickly become very hoarse. Singing quietly should actually use your support muscles at least as much as when singing *forte* (*f*).

Musical Terms

A written piece of music can contain lots of information – not just the notes to be sung and in what rhythm, but *how* to sing them.

Articulation Marks
(tell a singer how to sing the notes, e.g. smoothly or with an accent)

♩ (accent) – sing with an accent

legato – sing smoothly

♩ ♩ ♩ (slur) – sing the marked notes smoothly

♩ (*staccato*) – sing these notes detached, short and crisp

♩ (*tenuto* (*ten.*)) – slightly lengthen and sustain the note

Did you know?

Articulation marks are usually put close to the note-heads.

Tempo Marks and other signs
(tell a singer what speed to sing the music and other details)

Andante – at a walking pace
Allegro – fast
Moderato – at a moderate pace
Adagio – slow
Allegretto – quite fast
Vivace – fast and lively
M.M. ♩ = **92** – metronome markings
⌢ (pause mark) – hold the note or rest a little longer than usual

| 1. | first time bar |

| 2. | second time bar |

ritardando (**rit.**) – getting slower

‖: :‖ (repeat marks) – repeat the section or repeat from the beginning of the piece

Handy tip

Tempo marks are usually put above the music at the beginning of a piece.

Expression Marks
(tell a singer what kind of feeling/mood to give the music)

cantabile – with a singing tone
espressivo – expressively
grazioso – gracefully
molto – very (*molto espressivo* means 'very expressively')

Handy tip

Expression marks are usually put above the stave in most vocal music, so that they don't get in the way of the lyrics.

Manuscript Paper

Use this page to write down any exercises or ideas to help you.

Afterword

I hope that some of these tips have been useful to get you going and enjoying singing. These exercises and songs are designed to help you to free your voice and feel more confident. Please don't try to take it all in at once, or think that you are 'not doing it right'!

Singing is a basic human need and your voice has enormous expressive potential that you use every day when speaking. We are just extending that further here into the realm of music. Don't let people say you can't do it. Whether you sing in the shower or on Broadway, we're all singers and that's that.

Remember

We are the lucky ones! We take our voices with us the whole time! We can sing wherever and whenever we want! We look forward to hearing you!